APOCALYPSE MIAOW MIAOW

James Proimos III

illustrated by
James Proimos Jr.

BLOOMSBURY
LONDON   OXFORD   NEW YORK   NEW DELHI   SYDNEY

To the Maryland SPCA for taking good care of Brownie before he found a home with us —James Proimos III

For Bugga —James Proimos Jr.

Bloomsbury Publishing, London, Oxford, New York, New Delhi and Sydney

First published in Great Britain in November 2015 by
Bloomsbury Publishing Plc
50 Bedford Square, London WC1B 3DP

First published in the USA in November 2015 by
Bloomsbury Children's Books
1385 Broadway, New York, New York 10018

www.bloomsbury.com

Bloomsbury is a registered trademark of Bloomsbury Publishing Plc

Text and illustration copyright © Welcome Literary LLC 2015

The moral rights of the author and illustrator have been asserted

A CIP catalogue record for this book is available from the British Library

ISBN 978 1 4088 5685 7

Printed and bound in Great Britain by CPI Group (UK) Ltd, Croydon CRO 4YY

The
Prologue

1

Something very, very odd was going on out in the world.

The kooks who made outlandish predictions suddenly seemed far less kooky.

Humans vanished from moving vehicles.

But inside this house, a team of ragtag heroes had formed. Yes, in the past they had lost a battle or two, but now they were ready for anything!

Scene
One

19

Scene
TWO

Scene
Three

28

He sorta ran off.

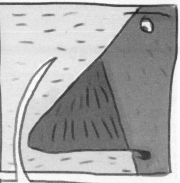

He don't see so good. I bet it was our person.

He may know what's going on. He may know where all the other people are.

And where more food is.

We are all out!

Scene
Four

34

Scene
Five

37

The Rat

And that just happened to be the night our last stash of food vanished!

43

I would do
anything
for the
team.
I would give
you the
shirt off
my back!

The shirt off
my back!

For those of you not in the know, a Twonkie is a tiny snack cake filled with sugary goo.

49

Scene
Six

Scene
Seven

There is a kitty cat in there. All you have to do is chase him out.

That's it?

C'mon guys, we are going in.

Scene Eight

Scene
Nine

Scene
Ten

Scene
Eleven

Scene
Twelve

The angry dog had got his pals in a terrible fix, but he did take the lion up on an offer to enjoy what the rat later called "Our Last Meal-a-thon"—a swimming pool that had been emptied of water and filled with thousands upon thousands of Twonkies.

The Belly Flop

The Synchronised Dive

Scene
Thirteen

Scene
Fourteen

*See your copy of *Apocalypse Bow Wow* or buy a copy now!

Wow. I could never be sick of Twonkies.

I bet you are one of those fancy Twonk-a-doodle dogs.

Well, you are what you eat.

Scene
Fifteen

Scene
Sixteen

ROUND 3 | WINNER! | LOSER!
ROUND 4 | WINNER! | LOSER!
ROUND 5 | WINNER! | LOSER!
ROUND 6 | WINNER! | LOSER!
ROUND 7 | WINNER! | LOSER!
ROUNDS 8–52 | WINNER! | LOSER!

ROUND
53

Scene
Seventeen

Too energised to go right to sleep, the angry dog asks the silly dog to take a walk with him.
This is fun!

Scene Eighteen

That night, the tough dog went to bed certain that all was lost. But at about 3 a.m., a simple yet brilliant plan came to him in his sleep and woke him up.

The first thing he did was
wake up the cop and tell
him the plan.

Psst
Psst

The cop told the cat.

Psst
Psst
Psst

153

Scene
Nineteen

159

160

Scene Twenty

FLICK

183

Plan B was supposed to be all of us attacking the lion at once, but now we are only three. Should we abort?

Not a chance. This was always a long shot.

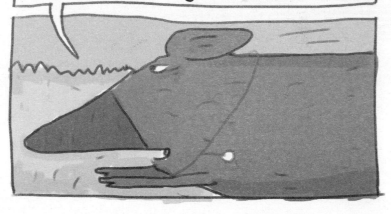

189

THE END

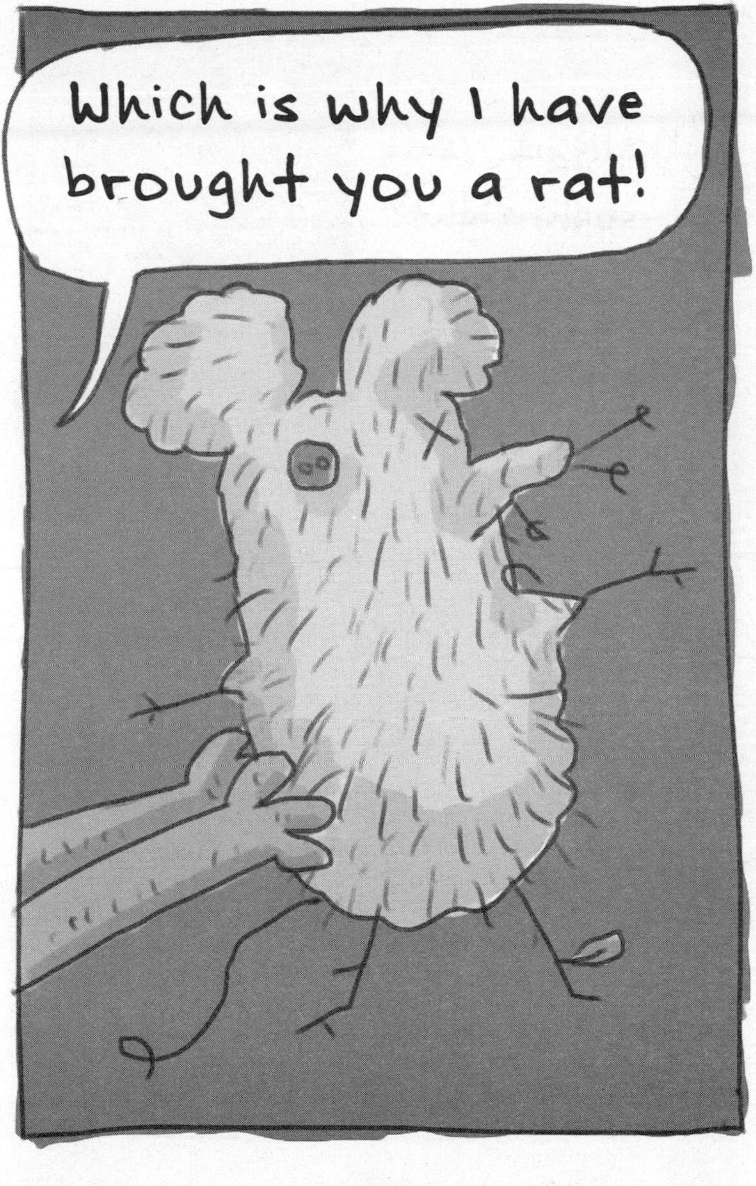
Which is why I have brought you a rat!

Oh wait.

I bet that we all ate so many Twonkies that we taste like Twonkies now.

Like they always say, you are what you eat, Lion.

Scene
Twenty-two

The gang made it down from the tree but had no idea what had happened until the silly dog explained it all . . .
. . . And then the lion just left.

Step Two:
We took the sugary goo and squished it together to form the perfect shape of a rat.

Step Three:
We added eyes.

(button)   (pebble)

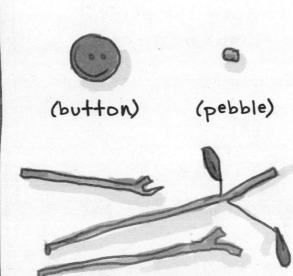

And legs and arms
(branches).

Step Four:
We added lots of rat hair!

Scene
Twenty-three

James Proimos III

Can two dogs survive the end of the world?

APOCALYPSE
BOW WOW

A hilarious graphic
novel illustrated by
James Proimos Jr

BLOOMSBURY